CW00385283

PRAYERS
FOR THE
FAMILY

*Also by John Woolley
and published by Arthur James*

I Am With You

Sorrow Into Joy

God's Secret

The Friendship of Jesus

Words of Power

PRAYERS
FOR THE
FAMILY

John Woolley

ARTHUR JAMES
JOHN HUNT PUBLISHING
NEW ALRESFORD
1999

First published in Great Britain in 1999 by

ARTHUR JAMES
an imprint of
JOHN HUNT PUBLISHING
46a West Street, New Alresford, Hants SO24 9AU
United Kingdom

The author would like to thank John Lynch and Philip Law
for help in the preparation of this book.

John A. Woolley asserts the moral right
to be identified as the author of this work.

A catalogue record for this book is available
from the British Library.

ISBN 0 85305 449 5

Typeset in Adobe Goudy by
Strathmore Publishing Services, London N7

Printed and bound by
Tien Wah Press, Singapore

Contents

Preface   vii

Family Prayers   1

On My Own   37

Preface

Talking to God isn't always easy!

With families in mind, this is a collection of prayers which older and younger can use together, in order to help an enjoyable and meaningful prayer-time to be a regular feature in many homes. One suggestion is to take it in turns to read.

After the Family Prayers there is a collection of very short prayers – 'On My Own' – which boys and girls may say alone (or with a little help from an adult, or a big brother or sister!)

After a month we can start again with Day 1.

Once we have begun the good habit of talking with Jesus every day – letting Him speak quietly into our hearts – we find ourselves feeling closer and closer to Him.

May this be true for everyone using this little book.

JOHN A. WOOLLEY
London, January 1999

Making Us

At the very start, God made the heavens and the earth.
                              – *Book of Genesis*

God our Father, although we can't see You, we wish we could!

We know that you are all around us; everywhere we go, You are with us.

Your world has so many wonderful things in it:
  beautiful rivers …
  trees …
  mountains …

And so many people who are really kind.

Because You made everybody and everything You must be a wonderful Person.

Thank You for making us.

DAY 2

Showing Us

Jesus said: 'If you look at me, you're looking at God.'
— *St John's Gospel*

God our Father, however hard we look, we can't see You. Lots of people would love to know what You look like.

A long time ago, You thought of a very clever way to show us what You are like. You became one of us! This was when Jesus came to the earth.

When people looked at Jesus they could see You; they could see how much You love us; they saw how You can do *everything*.

Thank You, God, for showing us what You are really like.

God Lived Among Us

God said: 'I will come and live with you.'
— Book of Zechariah

Lord Jesus, help us to remember, often, how You were born in a dirty, smelly old stable in Bethlehem.

There was no room for Mary and Joseph and their new baby, except where the animals lived.

Lord Jesus, You are God's present to the world; the best present we've ever had.

You came to make so many sad people smile again. You came very quietly – only a few knew about it.

There was no room for You at the inn. But there'll always be room for You in our hearts.

DAY 4

Sharing with Us

Jesus said: 'I am the Light for the whole world.'
— *St John's Gospel*

Lord Jesus, we thank You that God the Father made all the world through You.

Thank You for coming to share our lives with us. You are like a very bright light, shining in the dark so that we don't get lost.

Lord Jesus, You know all about us – the good things and the bad things – but You go on loving us all the time.

Since You were on the earth You know just how *we* feel – even though You are God.

We want You to be our Friend – always.

DAY 5

Listening to Us

'Never stop praying.'
– St Paul

Lord Jesus, You have so many children who forget to talk to You.

When we love someone, it makes us sad if that person stops talking to us. That is how You must feel when we forget You. Please don't let us be like that.

Dear Lord, we will try to speak to You about everything that happens to us, because You know what to do to help us.

Even if we can't always think of just what to say, when we pray, You're still glad, because we are thinking about You.

There are lots and lots of minutes in each day. Help us to remember to use some of them to be with You and talk to You.

Just Look at That!

The people were amazed and said: 'Jesus does everything well.' – St Mark's Gospel

Lord Jesus, thank You for the wonderful things which You did for people, which we can read about in our Bible.

You gave us a very special look at God doing things. What You did made people say: 'Just look at *that*!'

Help us to read our Bible just as if we were *right by You* when You did all those wonderful things …

    watching people who had never walked start jumping about.

    hearing people who had been blind say, 'Oh thank You, Jesus' when they opened their eyes and saw You.

Lord Jesus, nobody else could help those blind, deaf and crippled people. But *You* could, because You are God. You even made dead people live again.

Thank You for the marvellous things which You did, and the wise words which You said. Show us what it means for us, today.

DAY 7

So Brave

On the Cross, Jesus said: 'Father, forgive them; they do not know what they are doing.'
— St Luke's Gospel

Lord Jesus, to show how much You love us, You even let those people kill You. You did it so that we could belong to You for ever.

Thank You for being so brave on the Cross – that's why brave people today wear medals which are shaped like Your Cross. The Cross is Your special sign; it shows everybody that we are on Your side.

On the Cross You even went on loving those who did that terrible thing to You.

Thank You, Lord, for being so loving and so brave – all for us. I want to be Yours for ever.

DAY 8

Easter Sunshine

When the disciples saw Jesus, they were so happy.
                              – St John's Gospel

Not just in March or April, but *every* day in the year, help us to thank You, Lord Jesus, for Easter.

You made the darkness turn bright for everybody. When You died on the Cross, it was like a big black cloud over the world. But behind the cloud, the sun was shining all the time!

You came back to us alive. You said 'hello' to Your friend Mary, and to all the others. Lord Jesus, You couldn't stay dead for ever because You're God!

Before You went back to heaven, You said You would always be with us – even if we couldn't see You. Easter has changed everything!

DAY 9

Just Us!

God said: 'I hear all your prayers.'
– Book of Jeremiah

Lord Jesus, we do thank You for each time we can be together and think about You.

Thank You for the times when we can tell You just how we're feeling.

We'll always try to tell You the truth, and not try to hide anything from You. Each time we talk to You it helps us, so we'll try to find lots of times to talk to You.

When we've said a prayer about something, help us not to give up if You don't send what we want straight away. Help us to know the right things to ask for.

Talking to You makes *us* feel better, and makes *You* very pleased. So we won't forget …

Inside Us

Jesus said: 'Let Me live in you.'
— St John's Gospel

Lord Jesus, it's no use just trying to *copy*
You. You showed us a better way than that
– a secret way. You told us that You can
live inside us, helping us to grow more like
You.

Every time we read about You
    or talk to You
    or even just think about You
there's a little bit more of *You* inside us,
    helping us to like what You like,
    helping us to be kind like You are.

Lord Jesus, thank You that when You live
inside us we become more and more like
You – even if we don't notice it!

Thank You that we know the secret of
being more like You.

People Who Don't Like Us

Jesus said: 'I want you to say a prayer for people who are unkind to you.'
— *St Matthew's Gospel*

Lord Jesus, sometimes things happen which we're frightened to tell anyone about. Sometimes there are boys and girls – and grown-ups too – who don't seem to like us very much. They may say unkind things to us sometimes, and this makes us feel all alone or frightened of them.

You understand why people behave as they do. Help us to remember to say a prayer for them.

Lord Jesus, help us to remember that You are with us, that You are all around us, especially when we feel alone or afraid. Don't let us forget that *You* never stop loving us; then the other things won't matter nearly as much!

Trusting

God said: 'I made you, and will never forget to help you.'
— *Book of Isaiah*

Dear Lord, even a very good friend can forget about us sometimes … Even a good friend can be unkind sometimes …
But You are a very *special* friend …
You're somebody we can *trust*. Help us to remember that word of five letters.

Jesus, You *never* forget about us. You always send what is best for us at just the right time. You are making things happen for us even if we can't see them straight away!
You are all that a good friend should be … and lots *more*.

Each day we'll tell You how much we trust You. Each day we'll thank You that You never let us down. We want You to be in *every* part of our life.

DAY 13

Lots of Thank You's

'Thank God for everything.'
— St Paul

Dear Lord, very happy people seem
to have a secret. They are always saying
'Thank You' for something. So many people
forget to thank You for what they enjoy.

If we say 'Thank You' for some nice things
we will start to see lots of other nice things
as well!

Help us to start looking at some of the
things which You made:
    the stars,
    beautiful trees (even in the town!),
    lovely flowers,
    the sky,
    the fluffy clouds,
    the mountains and rivers …
        and lots more.

We'll try not to want what other people have got – because we can enjoy so many things ourselves.

We'll make You happy by saying lots of Thank You's every day.

DAY 14

Just to Please You!

Jesus said: 'If you do the things which I tell you, you're like the wise man who built his house on the rock.'
— *St Matthew's Gospel*

Lord, there are so many kind things which we could have done – but didn't!

There are so many wrong things we do which You would have helped us *not* to do.

We could have pleased You much more.

Jesus, Lord, if we think a lot about You, and talk to You, it will help us to stop thinking or saying or doing things which make You sad. We'll remember You inside us!

When we really *want* to do things which please You, we know that You'll always make us strong to do them.

Not Very Well

'I am God – who makes you well.'
— *Book of Exodus*

Lord Jesus, You are just like:
   a good doctor,
   a good friend,
   a good mum,
   a good dad,
… all rolled into one!

When we're not feeling very well, help us
to talk to You quietly on our own.

We know that because You love us, You
give us kind friends and good medicine to
make us better again.

Whenever we have to stay in bed, we won't
forget to say a prayer for old people who are
ill or lonely … boys and girls who are ill …
everyone *You* know who is feeling poorly
or sad.

DAY 16

Frightened

Jesus said: 'Do not be afraid … I'll always be with you.'
— *St Matthew's Gospel*

Lord Jesus, You know that people often feel a bit frightened … about all sorts of things.
Some are frightened of the dark
or of cruel people,
or of very fierce dogs,
or of thunder and lightning,
or of being alone in the house.

You know the things which frighten *us* most.

When we're frightened we'll try to remember just to whisper Your name … 'Jesus'. We'll remember that You're right there with us.

We'll feel braver if we think about You.

DAY 17

Secret Partner

Jesus said: 'I'm like the vine tree – you are the branches.'
— St John's Gospel

Lord Jesus, You don't just sit there watching us trying hard!

If we want to do a thing properly, You will always *help* us. If we want to help somebody, *You* make us strong.

When people thank us for doing something, they don't always know the secret of who's been helping us …
   When *I* try …
   and *You* help…
that's when we can do things really well.

Jesus, You love to be part of the things we do for people.

Please let us help a lot of people – together.

Your Help Is Special

God said: 'I will help all the sad ones who have no one to help them.'
        – Book of Zephaniah

Lord Jesus, when we say a prayer for somebody, we'll remember that all the world is in Your hands, we'll remember how much You love people.

You know *which* people need help very much, right now.

You know:
>   those who have lost somebody they love,
>   those with no job or no money,
>   those with nowhere to live,
>   those who are very ill or frightened,
>   those who feel nobody wants them,
>   those with not enough to eat,
>   those who find it hard to believe in You.

Lord, please use our prayers to let them feel that You are near them, and to feel Your love for them.

We promise to pray, often, for people we know, and for sad people everywhere.

Help us to *notice* those who seem unhappy, and help us to be kind to them.

DAY 19

I'd Like To Be …

Jesus said: 'I want you to be like a light shining for the people all around you.'
– St Matthew's Gospel

Lord Jesus, there are so many jobs we can do:
  a doctor, a nurse,
  a teacher, a vicar,
  a pilot, an engineer,
  a scientist, an artist,
  a TV presenter, a writer.
Hundreds of jobs …

Our job may one day be being a good mum or dad looking after our children – which is very important.

Help us to talk to You, often, about what we would like to do, and You will give us a feeling inside us about the sort of things You would like to see us do. And You will give us a feeling inside us about any job

which You *don't* really want us to do!
Lord Jesus, You are just the right person to
know the jobs which help people – and
which make *us* happy at the same time.
You know what each one of us can do best.

Using the Moments

God said: 'Come and meet Me.'
— Book of Psalms

Lord Jesus, when we've nothing much to do, when we're riding in a bus or train, or standing in a queue, when we're having a little sit-down somewhere … we know that You love us to talk to You. Every day has lots of times when we can do this.

In those few minutes we can say a prayer for somebody we know. We can tell You if we're worried about anything, we can thank You for some of the nice things in Your world. Help us to talk to You each morning, and lots of times in between!

Jesus, You are thinking about us all the time. We promise not to forget about You. Each time we talk to You, You're glad, because here is one more person who hasn't forgotten You!

DAY 21

Let It Be Me!

*Jesus said: 'If you are kind to people in
need, you are really being kind to Me.'*
— *St Matthew's Gospel*

Lord Jesus, help us to be kind to *everyone*
– not just those we like, or those who do
things for us. Let us love people like *You* do.

If we are kind to somebody, or even just
give them a smile, it can make them happy
for the rest of the day. When we are being
kind to a person, You told us that *You* feel
it as well. We are being kind to *You*!

When we help somebody, or try to cheer
them up, that happy feeling we get inside
comes from You.

Every day there are so many people we can
be kind to – and make *You* glad at the same
time.

Not Alone

*God said: 'I am with you wherever
you go.'*
                              – Book of Joshua

Jesus, Lord, there are times when people feel very lonely, when they feel that nobody cares about them.

It can happen at work, or school. It can even happen at home.

We may feel a bit scared of going somewhere or of seeing somebody. It doesn't really matter, because You will be there when we get there!

DAY 23

Oh Dear ...

*'I am your God – always kind, and ready
to forgive.'*
                                    – Book of Exodus

Lord Jesus, we're really sorry for wrong
things we have said or done – things which
hurt You. We haven't always tried our best.
You would have made us strong if we had
tried harder.

Because Your love is so *big*, we'll never be
afraid to come to You quickly and say we're
sorry. When we're *really* sorry, You are
pleased, and You forgive us straight away.
You help us to feel better again.

Please help us to do the same for other
people – to make friends after a quarrel,
not to hurt anyone, or try to pay them back.
We'll say a prayer for them instead.

Lord Jesus, Your way is the *best* way ...

DAY 24

Choosing

Jesus said: 'Follow Me!'
– St Mark's Gospel

Lord Jesus, all through our lives we have
to choose ... We have to choose:
   our job,
   where to live,
   what to buy.

You know how hard it is to choose one
cake from a plate of delicious cakes when
I can only have one! If we find it hard to
choose to be good when it's easier to do
something bad, we can say to ourselves:
'What would Jesus do now?'

The biggest choice we have to make is:
'Shall I live with Jesus as my Friend ... or
live without Him?'

Lord, we choose right now that we will
always share life *with* You!

DAY 25

Each New Day

God said: 'I will make you strong.'
                              – Book of Judges

Lord Jesus, thank You for every new day –
we'll share each one with You. Thank You
that it will be You and us *together*:

> when we feel weak,
>   You'll make us strong;
> when we don't feel like doing something,
>   You'll help us;
> when we feel like telling a lie,
>   You'll help us to tell the truth;
> when we feel like not being very nice to
>   somebody,
>   You'll help us to be kind, instead.

Lord Jesus, we promise to give You every
new day for You to use. Together we can
make it a good day every day!

DAY 26

Getting Dark

I will lie down and sleep peacefully.
– Book of Psalms

Lord Jesus, thank You for caring for us so wonderfully through each day. You save us from all sorts of dangers – some we don't even notice.

Each night, before getting into bed, it's nice to think about You:
    how much You love us …
    how great You are.

At the end of each day please show us where we have been wrong and help us to do better the next day.

Help us to use the little evening prayer, printed later in the book, every bedtime.

May our heavenly Father bless and keep us, His children, this night and for ever.

All Good Gifts

God said: 'I will be good to my children.'
– Book of Jeremiah

Jesus, Lord, if we peep inside a church in September or October we may see just how good You are to us!

At harvest-time we can spot:
    huge melons and rosy apples,
    delicious jam,
    black and green grapes,
    chunky fruit-and-nut bars,
    flowers of all colours,
    big loaves and chocolate cakes.

Thank You, Jesus for all these, and for other gifts like medicine for when we're poorly, wood for making lots of things, and petrol to make our cars go.

Help us to make *every* day like harvest-time – saying a big Thank You.

Tempted

Jesus said: 'Keep thinking about Me, so that you won't be tempted.'
                                    – St Matthew's Gospel

Lord Jesus, when we get to a crossroads, in a strange place, we don't always know which road to take.

When we do what pleases You, it's like taking the *right* road.

When we do something wrong, or let others tempt us, it's like taking a dangerous road, where we will be unhappy.

Dear Lord, help us to keep our eyes on You – and not go down any roads which will be bad for us, which will lead us to danger.

If we *let* You, You will save us from all sorts of dangers and dead ends. Thank You.

DAY 29

His Choice

Jesus said: 'You didn't choose Me; I chose you.'
                              – St John's Gospel

Lord Jesus, we talk to You and think about You because *You* chose us in the first place! You chose us so that You could look after us.

Even before we thought about You, You were thinking about us. You were right with us on the day that we were born – even *before* we were born.

If we trust You through our life we will see You one day as You really are – in Heaven. We won't need to guess about You any more.

Dear Lord, thank You for *choosing* us so that we get to know You more and more.

DAY 30

Jesus and Us

*God said: 'If you have Me, you have
everything you need.'*
— Book of Numbers

Lord Jesus, what a lot we've got if we've
got You!

You're the Light of the World ...
    helping us to see where we're going.
You're the Bread of Life ...
    making us strong and good.
You're the Good Shepherd ...
    keeping us safe.

We're so glad that You belong to us and we
belong to You!

Thank You.

Try These ...

Why not learn these prayers and say them every day?

Before a meal
For every cup, and every plateful,
Lord Jesus, make me truly grateful!

Before bed
God, my loving Father, hear me:
Bless me through this coming night.
Through the darkness You'll be near me,
Guarding me till morning light.

Getting up
God be in my eyes
And in my looking.
God be in my mouth
And in my speaking.
God be in my heart
And in my thinking.

And the very special one Jesus taught us

Our Father in heaven,
Hallowed be Your name.
Your kingdom come,
Your will be done,
On earth as it is in heaven.
Give us today our daily bread.
Forgive us for what we've done wrong,
As we forgive those who have done wrong
    things to us.
Take us away from temptation to do wrong.
Save us from all evil things.
For Yours is the Kingdom, the Power,
    the Glory,
For ever and ever! Amen.

On My Own

Here are prayers for each day of the month, which boys and girls can say on their own – or with a little help!

Some are easy to remember, so that we can say one or two without the book before very long.

DAY 1

Heavenly Father,

Thank You for making our world.
Thank You for making me.
You are with me wherever I go.
Thank You that You care for me.

DAY 2

God our Father,

Thank You for coming to us in Jesus. He showed us what You are like:

  so kind,
  so wise,
  so powerful.

Thank You.

DAY 3

Lord Jesus,

I know that You love me,
even when I've done something
wrong ...

You can help me when nobody
else can.

Please be my Friend for ever.

DAY 4

Lord Jesus,

It makes You sad
     when we don't talk to You,
because we know that You
     are always listening!

I will use the prayers
     in this book ...
and I'll make up
     some of my own as well!

DAY 5

Lord Jesus,

When I read my Bible I'll pretend
that I'm standing right by You …
when You did all those wonderful
things:

    making poorly people well
      again,
    making sad people happy again.

Only *You* could help those people.

DAY 6

Lord Jesus,

Thank You for being so brave on
    the Cross.
You did it because You love me.
You gave everything for me.
I give my heart to You.

DAY 7

Jesus, Lord,

Easter is a happy time
because it means You're alive!

You promised to be with us for
ever. I will remember this *every*
day of the year.

From Your home in Heaven You
watch over me – to keep me safe
until I see You one day.

DAY 8

Lord Jesus,

Because You know everything,
when I'm sad I can always talk to
You …

You help me to feel better again.

DAY 9

Lord Jesus,

If You are with me ...
    it doesn't really matter
    if some boys or girls are
        cleverer, or
        stronger
    than me.

I know that You will send me the
right friends – so that I can enjoy
being with them.

DAY 10

Lord Jesus,

Help me not to worry
when people say unkind things
to me.

Help me not to worry
about people who are not friendly
to me.

I will try to be friendly
    to everyone –
even if they are not always
    friendly back!

DAY 11

Lord Jesus,

Please make me more like You:
    brave …
    kind …
    wise …
    making other people happy.

Please live in me …

Thank You.

DAY 12

Lord Jesus,

When I'm afraid
I'll remember that:
    You are with me,
    taking care of me ...
    like a big strong wall
    all around me.

I know I can always be brave
when I am with You.

DAY 13

Thank You, Lord Jesus,

For everything You made:
    my home,
    food to eat,
    friends,
    music,
    birds singing,
    books to read ...
    and lots more.

A special thanks to You
for being my Friend –
and for being so good to me.

DAY 14

Lord Jesus,

When I forget You
    You don't forget me!

All the time
    You are thinking about me.

I know that I can trust You
    as my Friend for ever.

DAY 15

Lord Jesus,

Just to please You:
    I'll always keep my promises,
    I'll try not to feel sorry for
        myself,
    I'll try not to say unkind things
        to people or to have bad
        thoughts about them.

Still remembering You:
    inside me,
    helping me.

DAY 16

Lord Jesus,

When I'm poorly,
I know that You
want me to talk to You.

It will help me to be brave
and I will get better more quickly.

Thank You, Jesus.

DAY 17

Lord Jesus,

When I want to be good,
when I want to do something well,
You'll always help me.

Thank You, Jesus,
for all the times that it is
the two of us!

That's our secret ...

DAY 18

Jesus, Lord,

You knew how it felt to be lonely,
for people to be cruel to You.

When I feel all alone,
I know I'm not really ...

You are right by me!

DAY 19

Lord Jesus,

When I'm older,
help me to find a job
which pleases You.

I will talk to You
often about it
before I decide.

I know that if any job
helps other people
I will enjoy doing it.

DAY 20

Lord Jesus,

There are lots of people who are
    sad,
    poorly,
    or all alone.

I know that my prayers will help
them.

When I see anybody who seems
sad, I will be kind to them – for
Your sake.

DAY 21

Lord Jesus,

When I'm not busy, when I'm
sitting down for a few minutes,
I'll remember my promise to talk
to You …
> to tell You about anything
> > which I'm worried about;
> to thank You for caring for me;
> to pray for anyone I feel sorry
> > for.

You're always glad when I talk to
You!

DAY 22

Lord Jesus,

Show me every day how I can
help
    my family,
    my friends,
    and lots of others, too.

If I see
    a boy or girl who is
        looking sad,
    or a boy or girl whom
        nobody seems to like,
    or an old lady or old man
        looking very tired or lonely,
let *me* be the one to be kind to
them ...

DAY 23

Lord Jesus,

Help me to be *really* sorry for wrong things I have thought, said or done.

If I'm *really* sorry I know that You'll always forgive me.

I'll try to be like You and forgive.

I'll try to make friends again after a quarrel, and not try to pay people back.

DAY 24

Lord,

It's hard to choose, sometimes.

It's hard to choose to tell the truth when a lie would be easier.

It's hard to choose to do something extra for mum or a member of the family when I'm a bit tired or fed up.

When choosing is hard, I'll always say: 'What would Jesus do now?'

DAY 25

Lord Jesus,

Thank You for Christmas.

Thank You that You came from heaven to live with us.

You are God's special present to the world.

If I remember You, it will always be a happy Christmas.

DAY 26

Lord Jesus,

I will thank You, often, for all the good things in your world.

I'll remember to say a special prayer for boys and girls with not enough to eat.

Please help grown-ups to stop fighting each other ...

And to take care of Your children instead.

DAY 27

Lord Jesus,

Please help me to know when I'm starting to do something which hurts You.

Help me to stop straight away.

I remember Your promise that whenever I want to do what is right, You will make me strong.

DAY 28

Lord Jesus,

Thank You that You chose me.

You chose me to be somebody who follows You and who can love You more and more.

Thank You.

DAY 29

Lord Jesus,

As I talk to You every day,
I know that I will become:
    more sure of You with me,
    stronger …
    wiser …
    kinder …

As I talk to You every day,
I will enjoy it more and more …
And You enjoy it, too.

DAY 30

Lord Jesus,

Whatever I'm doing …
wherever I am …
whoever I'm with …

I can always remember that You're
there … caring for me.

Help me to remember to say lots
of little Thank You's every day.
This will help You and me to be
closer together.

Thank You!

TO SAY EACH MORNING

Thank You, Lord, for today.
You will be with me all the time.

You will help me
    to be kind to those I meet,
    to tell the truth,
    not to be miserable or
    feel sorry for myself.

You will show me when there is
danger.

Together we can have a good day,
every day!

Thank You.

TO SAY AT BEDTIME

Lord Jesus, thank You for looking after me today.

Thank You for my nice warm bed. I know You'll be watching me and keeping me safe through the night.

I'm sorry for the times I've hurt You; I promise to do better tomorrow.

Please bless boys and girls all over the world – specially those with no mum or dad.

Just before going to sleep, it's nice to think about You … how much You love me, how great You are.

TO SAY EVERY DAY

Lord Jesus, I know You love me because You died for me.

I'm sorry for the times I've hurt You.

I promise to be kind,
I promise to talk to You often.

Thank You for being so good to me.

I'm always going to be on *Your* side.

I'm going to trust You always!

Amen.

Also from John Woolley

I AM WITH YOU

Since 1984 people throughout the world have been discovering the power to change lives of the little devotional book, *I Am With You.*

The divinely inspired words bring a sense of our Lord's presence, in a wonderful way, to strengthen the reader in his or her personal need.

I commend this little book to all who are seeking to deepen their spiritual lives.
– Cardinal Basil Hume, England

I Am With You *is a very special book; it will bless countless people.*
– Prebendary John Pearce, England

I have never experienced such a closeness to Jesus.
– Fran Gunning, USA

A lovely book of devotions; we use it daily.
– Dr Donald English,
former president, Methodist Conference

I Am With You *will deeply touch many people.*
– Fr. Robert de Grandis, USA

The most wonderful book I have ever read.
– Fr. Tom Cass, England